Now I am Big

I Can Say These Words

by Gill Davies

Illustrated by Stephanie Longfoot

Brimax · Newmarket · England

sun

dinosaur

paint

Now we're big we go to school
And look at the pictures on the wall.

We can say the words that are with them;
Now we're big we know them all.

clock

truck

rainbow

slide

ball

shower

We like it at the swimming pool.
We paddle, splash and play.

It's lots of fun to play in the water.
We want to stay in here all day.

water wings

swimsuit

towel

baby

bag

buggy

We push the baby in the buggy
Along the busy street.

Mother stops and talks
To all the friends we meet.

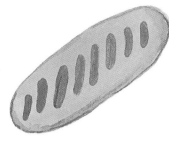

bread

dog

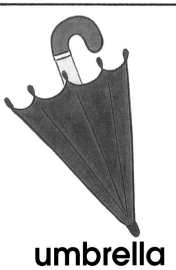

umbrella

mixing bowl

eggs

milk

We help mother and father in the kitchen,
Taking turns to stir the cake.

And we share the other chores
While we wait for it to bake.

apron

spoon

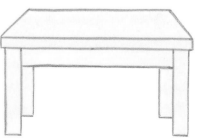

table

cards

presents

cake

"Happy Birthday!" we all sing.
Claire is four today.

She blows out the candles on her cake.
Now it's time to play!

candles

cookies

balloon

chair

hand

cushion

We share our new glove puppets;
We make them dance about.

When they jump and peek-a-boo,
The baby laughs and shouts.

puppet

goldfish

photograph

apple pie

banana

tree

Grandma takes us for a picnic.
We say, "That apple pie looks nice."

She shares it out between us
And gives everyone a slice.

flower

rabbit

bird

crayons

sky

paper

We are sitting outside today
And we draw what we can see.

I am drawing a great, big, yellow sun
In a sky as blue as can be.

swing

bicycle

pencil

mother

father

book

We give baby her first book.
She likes the pictures there.

Even when they are upside down,
They make her stop and stare.

cat

television

glass

lamp

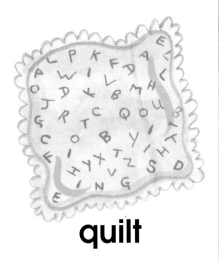

quilt

teddy bear

Our baby goes to bed early,
Mother kisses her on her cheek.